Town&Country
DOGS

HEARST BOOKS
A division of Sterling Publishing Co., Inc.

New York / London
www.sterlingpublishing.com

Library of Congress Cataloging-in-Publication Data
Town & Country dogs / from the editors of Town & Country.
p. cm.
ISBN-13: 978-1-58816-696-8 ISBN-10: 1-58816-696-1
1. Dogs--Pictorial works. 2. Dogs--Quotations, maxims, etc.
I. Town & country (New York, N.Y.) II. Title: Town and County dogs.
SF430T69 2008
636.7--dc22
2007045875

10 9 8 7 6 5 4 3 2 1

Published by Hearst Books
A Division of Sterling Publishing Co., Inc.
387 Park Avenue South, New York, NY 10016

Town & Country and Hearst Books are trademarks of Hearst Communications, Inc.

www.townandcountrymag.com

Design by Megan Rotondo
Jacket photos: cover by Julie Skarratt; spine by John Huba

Text by Susan K. Hom

For information about custom editions, special sales, premium and corporate purchases,
please contact Sterling Special Sales Department at 800-805-5489 or
specialsales@sterlingpublishing.com.

Distributed in Canada by Sterling Publishing
c/o Canadian Manda Group, 165 Dufferin Street
Toronto, Ontario, Canada M6K 3H6

Distributed in Australia by Capricorn Link (Australia) Pty. Ltd.
P.O. Box 704, Windsor, NSW 2756 Australia

Manufactured in China

Sterling ISBN 13: 978-1-58816-696-8
ISBN 10: 1-58816-696-1

❧ Introduction ❧

It's about time *Town & Country* went to the dogs. I say this in the most affectionate way. These four-legged creatures have been a part of the life of this magazine since its inception in 1846. Man's best friend, a woman's closest companion, and a kid's favorite pal—that's been a domestic dog's role. But it's not his or her only one. Canines have guarded, retrieved, rescued, hunted, stalked, and herded for centuries. Think of the Beagle, the German Shepherd, the St. Bernard, the Spaniel, and the Border Collie—all of them working dogs.

In the early days of *Town & Country*, pedigreed dogs were often photographed posing with their pedigreed owners, and it was sometimes hard to know who was the purer breed (probably the pooch).

In recent years, the canines of choice haven't always been so refined. As is true of today's wealthy in America, a dog doesn't need to be born rich to succeed. Hence the proliferation of mixed breeds (a.k.a. mutts) and hybrids (Labradoodles and the like) that the American Kennel Club looks at askance.

But no matter their lineage (or lack thereof), their size or their characteristics, dogs are the most lovable and lifelong of friends. See some winning examples from the pages of *Town & Country*. In our eyes, they are all Best in Show.

Pamela Fiori
Editor in Chief
Town & Country

The dog was created
specially for children.

·Henry Ward Beecher·

A dog is one of the remaining
reasons why some people can be
persuaded to go for a walk.

·O. A. Battista·

Maltese

Since ancient times, aristocrats have enjoyed coddling the silky, white Maltese in their arms. Named after the island of Malta in the Mediterranean, the Maltese has a gentle, sweet disposition that has charmed the hearts of such historical stalwarts as Publius, the Roman governor of Malta, and Queen Elizabeth I. Nicknamed the "comforter," this lap dog was placed on the chests of the sick by Elizabethan-age owners who believed that the Maltese possessed amazing healing powers. When he isn't warming laps, he loves to play.

The dog has no ambition,
no self-interest, no desire for
vengeance, no fear other than
that of displeasing.

·Georges-Louis Leclerc·

For me a house or an apartment
becomes a home when you add one
set of four legs, a happy tail, and
that indescribable measure of love
that we call a dog.

·Roger A. Caras·

English Springer Spaniel

This sporting dog is a pro at "springing" (flushing) and retrieving game on land and in water. The English Springer Spaniel is a good-natured family dog and is most happy when at his owner's side. English Springer Spaniel Ch. Felicity's Diamond Jim won Best in Show at the 2007 Westminster Kennel Club—the third Springer to take the title in less than fifteen years. The English Springer Spaniel is an active, gregarious fellow who puts his heart into his work and play, even if it's fetching socks for hours upon end.

The nose of the Bulldog has been slanted backwards so that he can breathe without letting go.

·Winston Churchill·

{ overleaf: Ella, Hopper, Harvey ❧ Bernese Mountain Dog (left, middle), Cavalier King Charles Spaniel (right) ❧ Courteney Cox ❧ Los Angeles }

Dachshunds are ideal dogs for small children, as they are already stretched and pulled to such a length that a child cannot do much harm one way or another.

·Robert Benchley·

Dogs love company. They place it
first in their short list of needs.

·J. R. Ackerley·

Saluki

The Saluki was revered and even mummified by the pharaohs in ancient Egypt. Elegant and regal, this hunter has a long, sleek body and gallops with great speed and stamina, tracking her prey by sight. Originally used by the Bedouin to hunt gazelle, the Saluki was later used by the British to bring down the agile hare. Today her grace, speed, and athleticism earn her prizes in the sport of lure coursing, which simulates the hunting of quick-footed prey.

The cat will mew, and dog
will have his day.

·William Shakespeare·

Our perfect companions never
have fewer than four feet.

·Colette·

Pug

The Pug, who originally heralds from China, is utterly charming, from her wrinkled muzzle down to her curly tail. Sometimes referred to as *multum in parvo*, or "much in little," she can be quite bold—like Fortune, Joséphine Bonaparte's pet, who was a secret message carrier. Joséphine hid notes for her husband, the Emperor Napoleon, under her dog's collar when she was held in the prison of Les Carmes. The Pug is usually forgiven for her excited grunting or loud snoring because she is a joy to be around and has a delightful sense of humor.

The psychological and moral comfort of a presence at once humble and understanding—this is the greatest benefit that the dog has bestowed upon man.

·Percy Bysshe Shelley·

I understand that most ladies tend
to prefer lap dogs. . . . Perhaps I am
an exception.

·Emily Brontë·

Pomeranian

The Pomeranian (or Pom) certainly doesn't act like a six-pound dog—perhaps the influence of her Eastern European bloodlines. She isn't afraid to confront large dogs and demand their attention with a bark that resembles a yip. The Pomeranian's alert nature makes her a perfect watchdog, and she is lively both in the show ring and at home. Queen Victoria's faithful Pomeranian, Marco, was a devoted companion, staying close by her feet until her death.

I can say on firsthand authority that Poodles do not like brandy; all they like is champagne and they prefer it in a metal bowl.

·James Thurber·

Men are generally more careful of
the breed of their horses and dogs
than of their children.

·William Penn·

A dog teaches a boy fidelity, perseverance, and to turn around three times before lying down.

·Robert Benchley·

Standard Poodle

In the Middle Ages, German hunters used the Standard Poodle as a duck retriever. An excellent swimmer, he got his trademark haircut in order to prevent joint injuries in the cold water. The Standard Poodle is refined, with a walk that exudes confidence and elegance. A social butterfly, he doesn't need a lot of "alone" time and is a quick learner. So adept and trainable is the Standard Poodle that his talents range from capable guard dog to entertaining performer to reliable retriever to outstanding companion.

If you don't own a dog, at least one,
there is not necessarily anything
wrong with you, but there may be
something wrong with your life.

·Roger A. Caras·

Labrador Retriever

The Labrador Retriever (or Lab) is known for his easygoing nature. The Lab's dependability makes him a sought-after worker, and he has been trained as both a guide and rescue dog. He excels as a sportsman's all-purpose retriever for his tenacity and soft mouth, and he has a distinct waterproof undercoat. His intelligence and agreeable disposition have made him a popular pet—in fact, he has held the number one spot in American Kennel Club breed rankings for more than ten years. There are black Labs, chocolate Labs, and yellow Labs, and people do seem to have their favorites.

The most affectionate creature in
the world is a wet dog.

·Ambrose Bierce·

{ Paco, Gina ❧ Chocolate Labrador Retriever, Jack Russell Terrier ❧
Giovanni Grendene ❧ Miami }

Dogs wait for us faithfully.

·Marcus Tullius Cicero·

Boxer

Early Boxer-type dogs can be found in stag-hunting scenes woven in sixteenth- and seventeenth-century Flemish tapestries. With a large, muscular body that gives him a powerful presence, the Boxer was originally used for the sports of dogfighting and bullbaiting. Today, his intelligence and alertness make him invaluable as both a service dog for the handicapped and a police dog. Often a puppy at heart, he is a loving family member with seemingly endless patience around children.

Acquiring a dog may be the only opportunity a human ever has to choose a relative.

·Mordecai Siegal·

{ overleaf: Olympe ⁂ Jack Russell Terrier ⁂ Luc Bouveret de Liance ⁂ Paris }

She was such a beautiful and sweet
creature . . . and so full of tricks.

·Queen Victoria·

Dalmatian

The Dalmatian has quite a résumé—and a beautifully spotted coat that is the envy of any room. Her intelligence, speed, and endurance make her a versatile worker, and she has been used to guide fire engine horses, act as a guard, and entertain in circuses. The Dalmatian needs lots of exercise and is the perfect match for an active owner. Ingrid Bergman and Eugene O'Neill both owned this breed, whose devotion is as noteworthy as her energy.

No one appreciates the very special
genius of your conversation
as a dog does.

·Christopher Morley·

My little dog—a heartbeat
at my feet.

·Edith Wharton·

Dachshund

The Dachshund's low and especially long body sets her apart in a crowd. Her lifespan is unusually long, too—up to seventeen years. Both the standard and miniature sizes of the Dachshund can have either a smooth, wirehaired, or longhaired coat. Originally bred in Germany to hunt for badgers, the Dachshund is clever and persistent. She loves to dig holes, often naughtily in pristine lawns and prized flowerbeds. The Dachshund has inspired many artists, from Leonardo da Vinci to Pablo Picasso, from William Shakespeare to P. G. Wodehouse.

No philosophers so thoroughly
comprehend us as dogs and horses.

·Herman Melville·

If you love to read, if you love
nature and if you have a dog, you've
got it made.

·Brooke Astor·

West Highland White Terrier

The West Highland White Terrier (or Westie)
keeps up her active schedule by indulging in
several daily naps. Originally bred as a hunter in
Scotland, the Westie's water-resistant double
coat allows her to fetch game in water, as well
as on land. The Westie loves to be showered with
attention. Full of charisma, this adorable terrier
was captured on the literary page by P. G.
Wodehouse in his novel *Jeeves and Wooster*.
A frequent main character in children's books,
the Westie has piercing black eyes and a black
button nose that have landed her in promotional
materials for everything from dog food
to cosmetics.

Great men have great dogs.

{ Puffin, Ratafià   Mix (both)   Paolo Pejrone   Revello, Italy }

Pomeranians speak only to Poodles,
and Poodles only to God.

·Charles Kuralt·

A Pekingese is not a pet dog; he is
an undersized lion.

·A. A. Milne·

Man himself cannot express love and humility by external signs so plainly as does a dog, when with drooping ears, hanging lips, flexuous body, and wagging tail, he meets his beloved master.

·Charles Darwin·

Jack Russell Terrier

Originally bred by the Reverend John Russell to be a fox hunter, the Jack Russell Terrier has a small chest that allows him to enter tight burrows. The Jack Russell Terrier's shorter legs make him distinct from the Parson Russell Terrier. There is an ongoing debate between the breeds' official American associations over which variation is closer to the Reverend John Russell's original vision for the breed and whether the Jack Russell and Parson Russell qualify as the same breed. But this doesn't bother the little guy at all! A loyal and enthusiastic companion, the Jack Russell Terrier has a feisty spirit and an expressive face.

I myself have known some
profoundly thoughtful dogs.

·James Thurber·

From the dog's point of view, his master is an elongated and abnormally cunning dog.

·Mabel Louise Robinson·

{ Archie, Cujo ❦ Maltese and Shih Tzu mix, Maltese ❦
Hilary and Bryant Gumbel ❦ New York City }

An animal's eyes have the power to
speak a great language.

·Martin Buber·

Old English Sheepdog

The Old English Sheepdog's agility and intelligence make her an excellent herder and family dog, rounding up both sheep and children. Never mind wet weather—her long, shaggy outercoat and water-resistant undercoat are perfect for working in the rain. The Old English Sheepdog is sweet and loyal to the end. Paul McCartney's Sheepdog inspired his song "Martha, My Dear."

Rambunctious, rumbustious,
delinquent dogs become angelic
when sitting.

·Ian Dunbar·

A puppy is but a dog, plus high spirits, and minus common sense.

·Agnes Repplier·

I have Social Disease. I have to
go out every night. If I stay home
one night I start spreading rumors
to my dogs.

·Andy Warhol·

{ overleaf: Otis, Gus ❧ Mix (both) ❧ Richard Donner ❧ Orcas Island, Washington }

If you eliminate smoking and gambling, you will be amazed to find that almost all an Englishman's pleasures can be, and mostly are, shared by his dog.

·George Bernard Shaw·

Siberian Husky

The Siberian Husky can be traced back to the
sled dogs of the Chukchi people of northeastern
Asia. Famous for his speed and stamina, the
Siberian Husky entered the American racing
scene in the All Alaska Sweepstakes Race of
1909. Unlike many breeds, the Siberian Husky
has a variety of eye colors, including solid
shades such as blue or brown and even
non-solid colors. The Siberian Husky is
outgoing but also independent.

Dogs are forever in the moment.
They are always a tidal wave of
feelings, and every feeling is some
variant of love.

·Cynthia Heimel·

Why, that dog is practically a Phi
Beta Kappa. She can sit up and beg,
and she can give her paw—I don't
say she will, but she can.

·Dorothy Parker·

Border Collie

The Border Collie comes from the "border" region between Scotland and England. Extremely intelligent, this breed can herd sheep with a firm stare called "eye." The Border Collie has a better grasp of human language than most dogs; she's able to understand phrases rather than just simple one-word commands. The Border Collie demands activity and attention, and thrives in dog sports like herding, agility, and fly ball. Her uncanny instincts also make her a great therapy dog.

A dog has the soul of a philosopher.

·Plato·

The more I see of men, the more
I admire dogs.

·Jeanne-Marie Roland·

German Shorthaired Pointer

The German Shorthaired Pointer (or GSP) is a true athlete who enjoys a vigorous workout. He will happily chase game or a flying disc. A versatile hunter, he is a good tracker and swimmer, with a keen sense of smell. Because he is such a stylish sportsman, the GSP has been featured in Ralph Lauren ads in which his good looks hold up to those of international models. This intelligent breed is quick, eager to learn, and comfortable around children. His warm, energetic disposition is ideal for an active family.

Dog. A kind of additional subsidiary Deity designed to catch the overflow and surplus of the world's worship.

·Ambrose Bierce·

The Pug is living proof that God
has a sense of humor.

·Margo Kaufman·

{ overleaf: Hoover ❖ French Bulldog ❖ John Boccardo and J.R. Roberts ❖ Palm Springs }

Golf seems to be an arduous way
to go for a walk. I prefer to take
the dogs out.

·Princess Anne·

Bulldog

Distinct from the French Bulldog, this warm and courageous breed is sometimes called the English Bulldog (though the breed's formal name is simply the Bulldog). Originally used as a bullbaiter, the Bulldog would hang on tightly to a bull with his undershot jaw. After the sport was made illegal in 1835, his vicious streak was bred out, and the Bulldog became a prized show dog and sought-after companion. President Calvin Coolidge's Bulldog was named Boston Beans. With his tenacious reputation (and distinctive appearance), it's no wonder the Bulldog is the mascot of more than a dozen American universities, as well as the symbol of the United States Marine Corps.

I am I because my little
dog knows me.

·Gertrude Stein·

{ Earl of Cork ❧ Corgi and Jack Russell Terrier mix ❧
Janet Mavec and Wayne Nordberg ❧ New Jersey }

To his dog, every man is Napoleon; hence the constant popularity of dogs.

·Aldous Huxley·

❧ Tidbits ❧

After we gathered the photos for this book, we contacted the dog owners with the news and were reminded just how much dogs really are a part of the family—how much they are loved and adored. Here a just a few of the responses we received, for you to enjoy:

❧ page 12 ❧

Rugby (left) was a stray who one day sidled up to a cowboy on Ralph Lauren's ranch in Colorado. Ralph eventually adopted the lucky pooch, who went from homeless to being master of many homes.

❧ page 34 ❧

When Lulu (right) was found on the streets of Queens, New York, she was starving and losing her hair. Now, thanks to the rescue group Bobbi and the Strays (bobbicares.petfinder.com), she's healthy and happy.

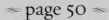

❧ page 50 ❧

Owner Alexis Swanson Traina wrote to us: "Thrilled to have the dogs included in your book!! I will tell them immediately. . . . Harvey (far left) is a mutt, discovered as a little puppy on Christmas Eve at the local grocery store in Napa Valley. Lafitte (near left) is a Wirehaired Dachshund named for the pirate Jean Lafitte." The photo was taken in the Swanson Vineyards Tasting Salon in Rutherford, California.

❧ page 62 ❧

Dede Wilsey let us know that Serena (right) was born with an enlarged heart and was expected to live no more than three years. She lived to be eleven because "she was so devoted to me and knew I needed her."

≈ page 72 ≈

This photo was taken in the library of owner Paulo Pejrone's home in Revello, Italy. Puffin (left) is a former stray dog, very old but very sweet and "simpatico." Ratafià (right) was born on August 11, 1999, and is "very, very clever and affectionate."

≈ page 80 ≈

According to owner Stiles T. Colwill, Sabrina (right) is "quite well and thrilled at being a star." In this photo, she's sitting in a labeled New York armchair made circa 1810 for the U.S. Capitol by Thomas Constantino.

≈ page 92 ≈

This litter of Dalmatian puppies (left) was up for adoption at the Bidawee shelter in Westhampton on Long Island, New York. They were all placed in loving homes after the photo was taken.

≈ pages 94 & 95 ≈

Otis (near right) is believed to be a Pit Bull and Labrador Retriever mix and was found in Foley Square in New York City. Gus (far right)—likely an Akita and Great Dane mix—was rescued on Orcas Island, Washington, where the photo was taken.

≈ page 112 ≈

Owner Bunny Williams tells us that Bubby (left) is a Dominican terrier who was "purchased from the local gas station for $20."

≈ page 120 ≈

We received this note from Janet Mavec: "Oh my, my, my. Our dog Cork (right) will be thrilled to know he is included in your upcoming book. His deceased sister was in *Vogue* many years ago, so he was worried about his own posterity."

Sources

Fogle, Bruce. *The New Encyclopedia of the Dog*. 2nd American ed. New York: Dorling Kindersley, 2000.

General Information Sites

American Kennel Club
www.akc.org

Canadian Kennel Club
www.ckc.ca/en

Dog Breed Info Center
www.dogbreedinfo.com

Just US Dogs
www.justusdogs.com.au

The Kennel Club
www.thekennelclub.org.uk

Pedigreedpups.com
www.pedigreedpups.com

PetPlanet.co.uk
www.petplanet.co.uk

The Westminster Kennel Club
www.westminsterkennelclub.org

Breed Specialty Sites

Border Collie
Border Collie Society of America
www.bordercolliesociety.com

Boxer
American Boxer Club, Inc.
http://americanboxerclub.org

Bulldog
The Bulldog Club of America
www.thebca.org

Dachshund
Dachshund Club of America, Inc.
www.dachshund-dca.org

Dalmatian
Dalmatian Club of America, Inc.
www.thedca.org

English Springer Spaniel
English Springer Spaniel Field Trial
  Association
www.essfta.org

German Shorthaired Pointer
German Shorthaired Pointer Club of America
www.gspca.org

Jack Russell Terrier
Jack Russell Terrier Club of America, Inc.
www.terrier.com

K9 Web
www.k9web.com/dogfaqs/breeds/jackrussells.html

Labrador Retriever
The Labrador Retriever Club, Inc.
www.thelabradorclub.com

Maltese

American Maltese Association
www.americanmaltese.org

Foxstone Maltese
www.foxstonemaltese.com/maltese_breed_
    history.htm

Old English Sheepdog

Old English Sheepdog Club of America,Inc.
www.oldenglishsheepdogclubofamerica.org

Parson Russell Terrier

Parson Russell Terrier Association of America
www.prtaa.org

Pomeranian

American Pomeranian Club, Inc.
www.americanpomeranianclub.org

Pug

Pug Dog Club of America, Inc.
www.pugs.org

Pugs.nl
www.pugs.nl

Saluki

Saluki Club of America, Inc.
www.salukiclub.org

Siberian Husky

Siberian Husky Club of America, Inc.
www.shca.org

Famous Huskies
http://users.tpg.com.au/users/cnicholl/
    famous_huskies.htm

{ Bubbie, Daisy ⋇ Cairn Terrier, Maltese ⋇ Thomas O'Brien ⋇ Bellport, Long Island }

Standard Poodle
The Poodle Club of America
www.poodleclubofamerica.org

Poodle History Project
www.poodlehistory.org

Standard Poodles USA
www.standardpoodlesusa.com

West Highland White Terrier
West Highland White Terrier Club of America
www.westieclubamerica.com

❧ Photo Credits ❧

Page 4 **Michael Mundy**
Page 6 **James Merrell**
Page 8 **Noe Dewitt**
Page 10 **Oberto Gili**
Page 12 **SKREBNESKI © 1996**
Page 14 **James Merrell**
Page 16–17 **Noe Dewitt**
Page 20 **Firooz Zahedi**
Page 22 **Oberto Gili**
Page 24 **Miki Duisterhof**
Page 26 **Chris Warde-Jones**
Page 28 **Oberto Gili**
Page 30 **Maura McEvoy**
Page 32 **Maura McEvoy**
Page 34 **John Huba**
Page 38–39 **John Huba**
Page 40 **Rob Howard**
Page 42 **Oberto Gili**
Page 44 **Julie Skarratt**
Page 46 **Matthew Gilson**
Page 48 **Noe Dewitt**
Page 50 **Robert Olding**
Page 52 **Rob Howard**
Page 54–55 **Alexandre Bailhache**
Page 58 **Melanie Acevedo**
Page 60 **John Huba**
Page 62 **Thayer Allyson Gowdy**
Page 64 **Fergus Greer**

Page 66 **Alexandre Bailhache**
Page 68 **Oberto Gili**
Page 70 **Miki Duisterhof**
Page 72 **Oberto Gili**
Page 76–77 **Fernando Bengoechea**
Page 78 **Miki Duisterhof**
Page 80 **Oberto Gili**
Page 82 **Oberto Gili**
Page 84 **Julie Skarratt**
Page 86 **Rob Howard**
Page 88 **Matthew Hranek**
Page 90 **Oberto Gili**
Page 92 **Anders Overgaard**
Page 94–95 **Marc Royce**
Page 98 **Priscilla Rattazzi**
Page 100 **Miki Duisterhof**
Page 102 **Jim Wright**
Page 104 **John Huba**
Page 106 **Rob Howard**
Page 108 **John Huba**
Page 110 **Matthew Hranek**
Page 112 **Brian Doben**
Page 114–115 **Tim Street-Porter**
Page 118 **Miki Duisterhof**
Page 120 **Gentl & Hyers**
Page 122 **Matthew Hranek**
Page 127 **Laura Resen**